CUT&
COLOR
PLAYBOOK
SEASONS

Anouck Boisrobert

CUT & COLOR PLAYBOOK
SEASONS

Kane Miller
A DIVISION OF EDC PUBLISHING

First American Edition 2016
Kane Miller, A Division of EDC Publishing

Copyright © 2016 The Ivy Press Limited

Published by arrangement with Ivy Press Limited, United Kingdom.

For information, contact:
Kane Miller, A Division of EDC Publishing
PO Box 470663
Tulsa, OK 74147-0663
www.kanemiller.com
www.edcpub.com
www.usbornebooksandmore.com

Library of Congress Control Number: 2015938832

Printed in China

ISBN: 978-1-61067-408-9

Safety warning: children should use craft scissors for the following
activities, and should be supervised by a responsible adult at all times.

CONTENTS

HOW TO USE THIS BOOK 6

WINTER

SPRING

SUMMER

FALL

MAKE YOUR OWN THREE-LAYERED SCENE 88

YOUR DESIGNS 96

HOW TO USE THIS BOOK

Color, cut & create four seasonal scenes!

1 Follow the instructions to add color and characters to the scene.

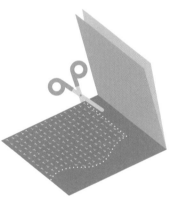

2 Cut away the parts of the pages that have a scissor pattern on the back.

3 Once you have colored and cut all the pages, flip back to the frame at the front to see the layered picture that is revealed. You can staple the edge of the pages to keep each scene together.

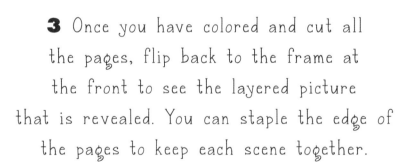

Tip: If you accidentally cut away the wrong part of the page, don't panic! Just fix it with some sticky tape on the back of the page.

HOW TO START

Poke your scissors into the hole that is
already cut out on the frame page, and start
cutting out the frame. Do this carefully to
make sure that you don't accidentally cut
into or break the frame.

Tip: Ask an adult to
help you if you find
 cutting out difficult.

WINTER

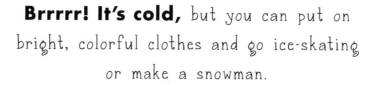

Brrrrr! It's cold, but you can put on bright, colorful clothes and go ice-skating or make a snowman.

Some animals sleep in the winter, but others find food to keep themselves warm. You can see foxes if you look carefully.

Lots of plants are asleep for the winter, but some trees and plants keep their dark green leaves all year round.

ith a pretty frame.

e foxes and trees.

utting here.

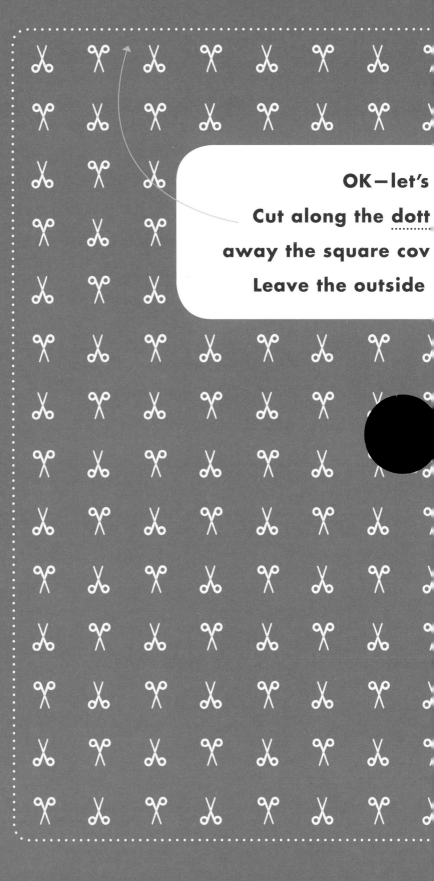

OK—let's
Cut along the dott
away the square cov
Leave the outside

Color in the rabbits.
Remember to leave their
fluffy tails white.

Here's a friendly snowman...
Color in the child and
the snowman. Don't forget
his orange carrot nose!

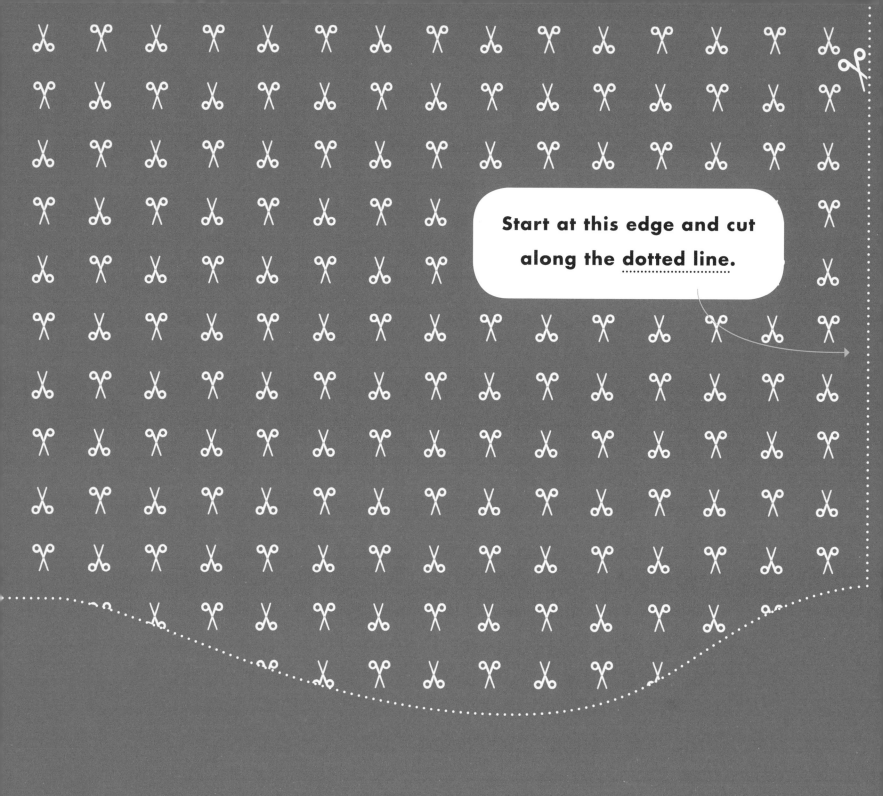

Whoosh...

Color in this daredevil sled rider.
And don't forget the birds!

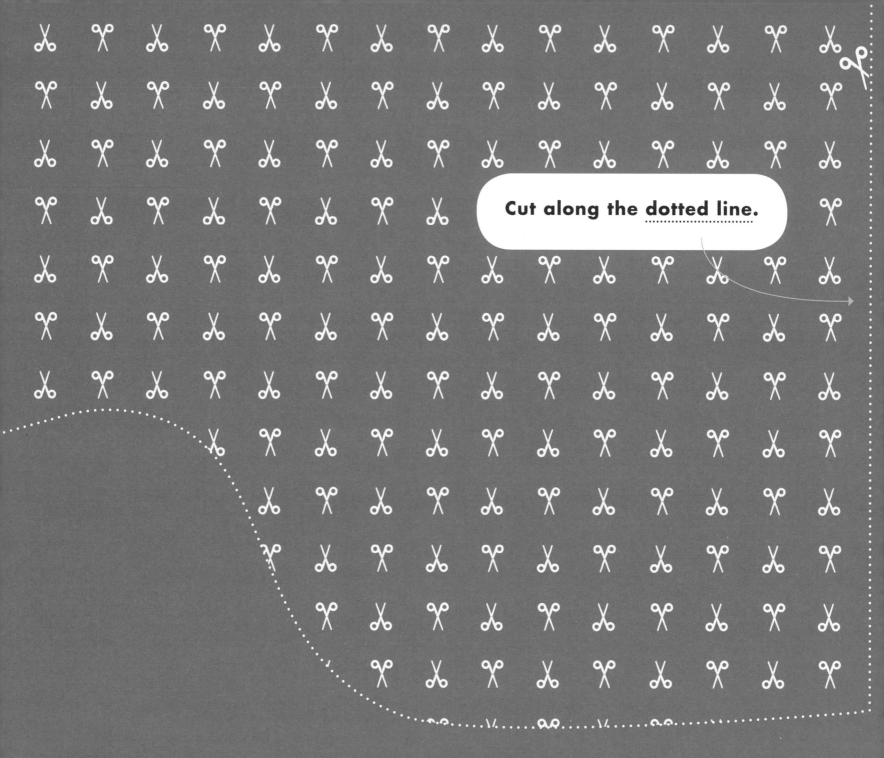

Cut along the dotted line.

This wintry tree has dark branches, but leave the ends a pretty snowy white.

Hoot hoot!
Color this owl's feathers brown.

Wheee!

Color this frozen lake an icy blue.

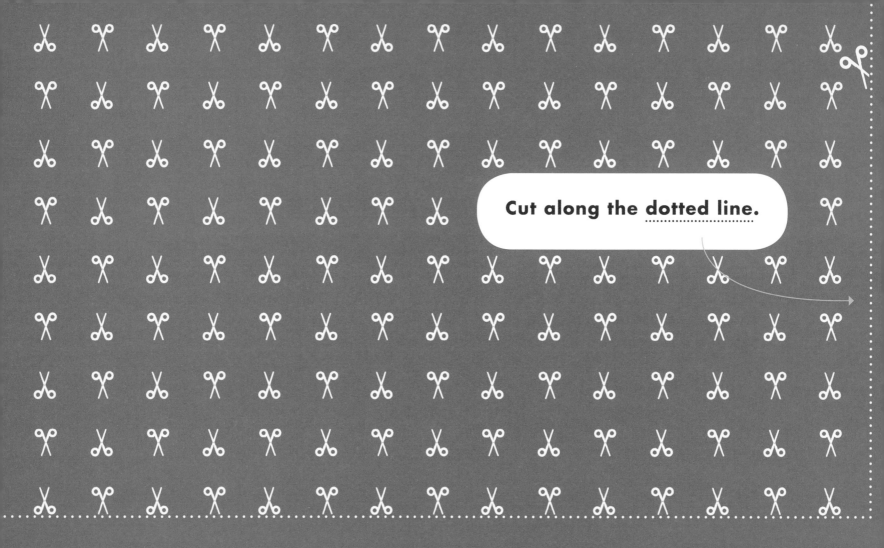

Cut along the dotted line.

This fox is watching the boy go
sledding. His fur is reddish brown,
but his neck and tail tip are white.

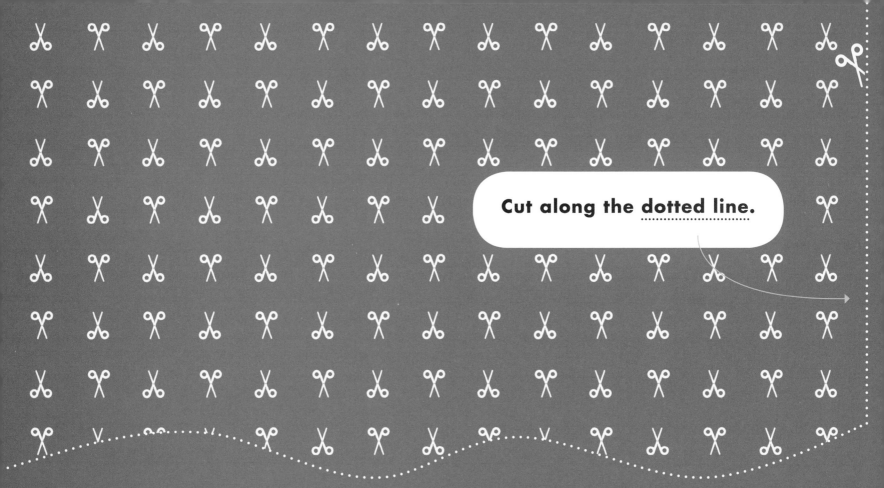

Cut along the dotted line.

Someone is at home!

What color will you paint the house?

Color these bushes green. The trees can also be green, but they can be lighter.

Cut along the dotted line, and snip away the triangles in the bushes.

Color in the trees
and the branches.

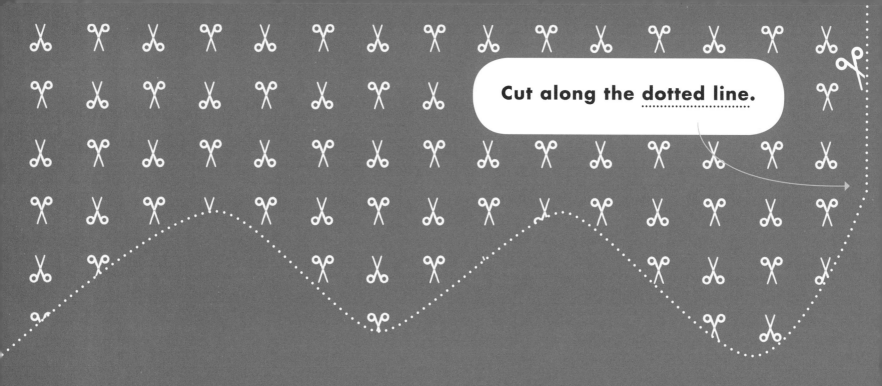

Cut along the dotted line.

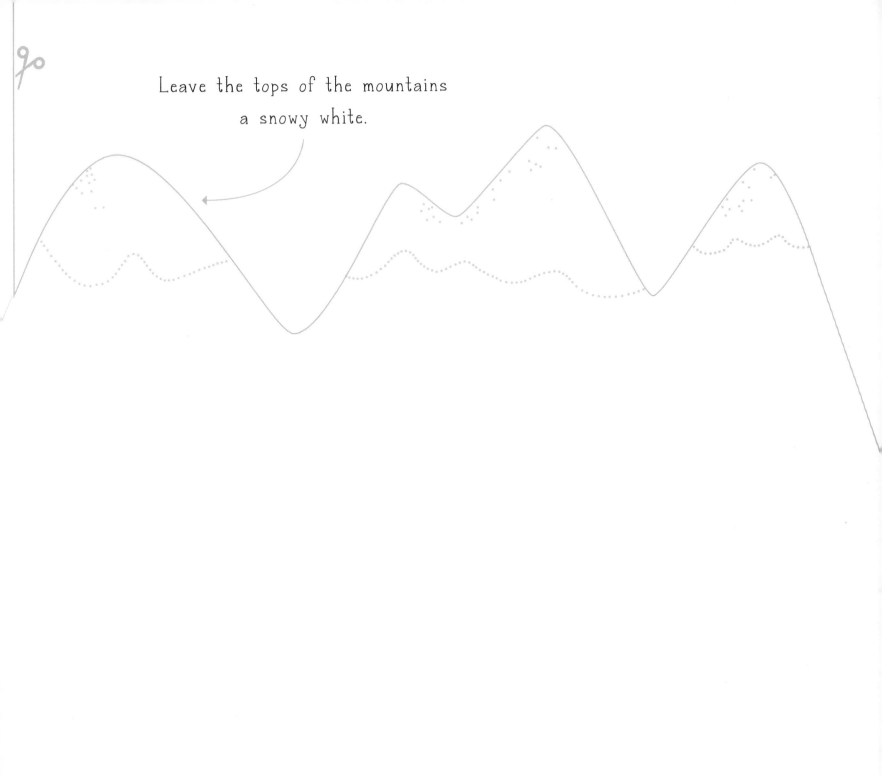

Leave the tops of the mountains
a snowy white.

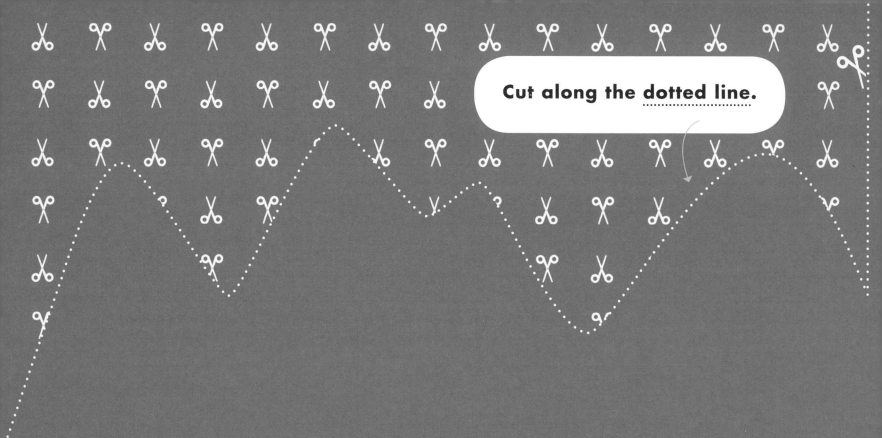

Cut along the dotted line.

SPRING

Spring is when leaves start to grow on trees and flowers come out. The flowers are often in bright and fresh colors.

Baby animals are born. Sometimes they are different colors from their mommies and daddies.

Butterflies come out to play in the warm sun. Their wings are often very pretty and have colorful patterns.

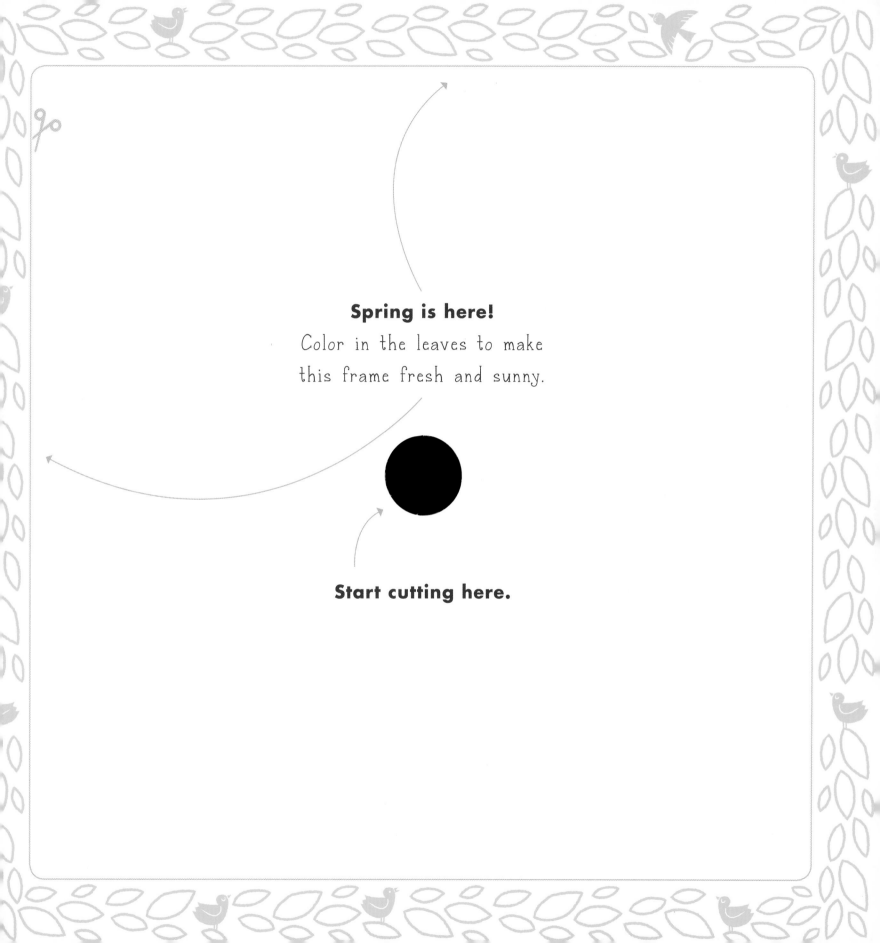

Spring is here!

Color in the leaves to make
this frame fresh and sunny.

Start cutting here.

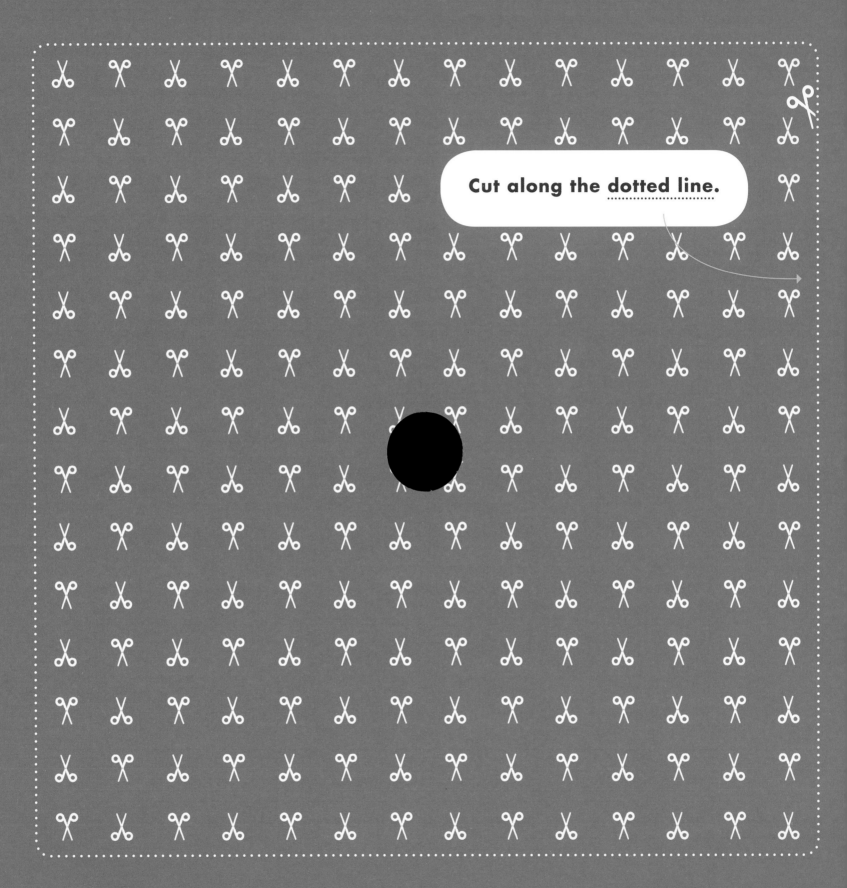

Cut along the dotted line.

Flutter...
Two butterflies have landed on the flowers.
Their wings shimmer in the sunlight.

Make these flowers really
bright and cheerful.

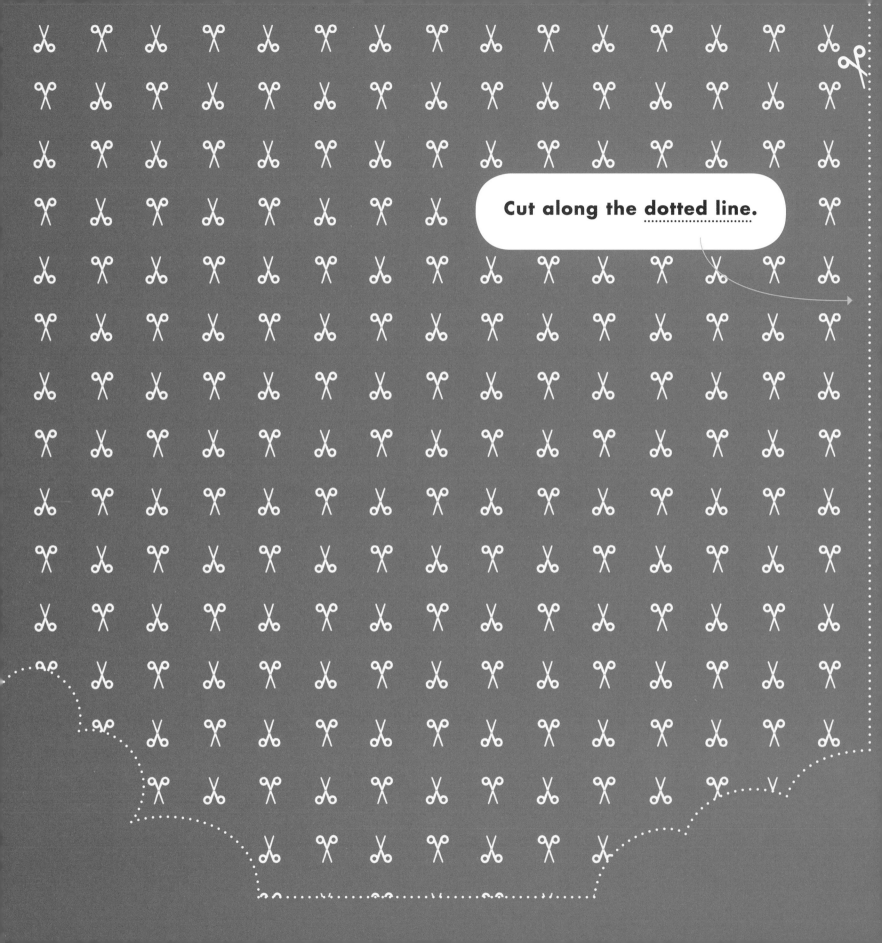

Cut along the dotted line.

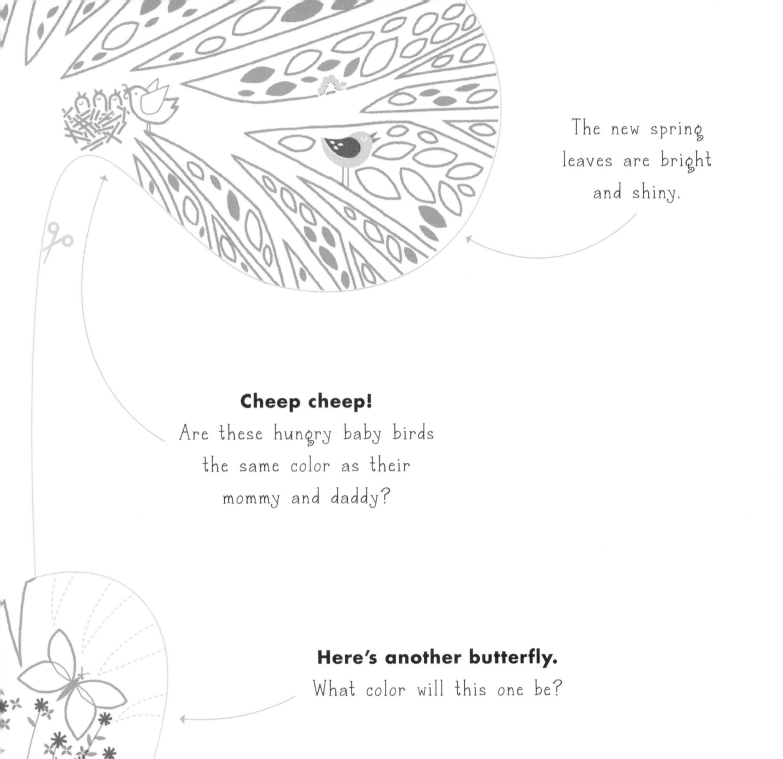

The new spring
leaves are bright
and shiny.

Cheep cheep!
Are these hungry baby birds
the same color as their
mommy and daddy?

Here's another butterfly.
What color will this one be?

Cut along the dotted line, and snip away the triangles in the bushes.

Quack quack! Splash!

One little duck has dived
under the water.

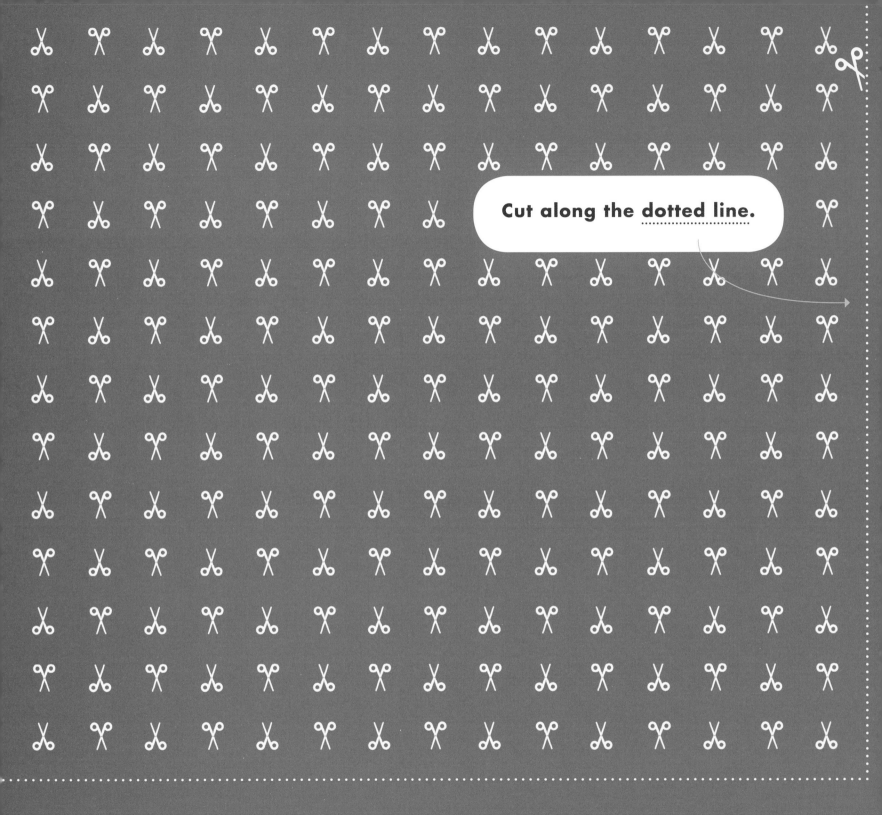

Cut along the <u>dotted line.</u>

Yum! It's picnic time!

What colors are you going to choose
for the little girl's hair and dress?

Can you see the wild flowers
on the grassy bank?

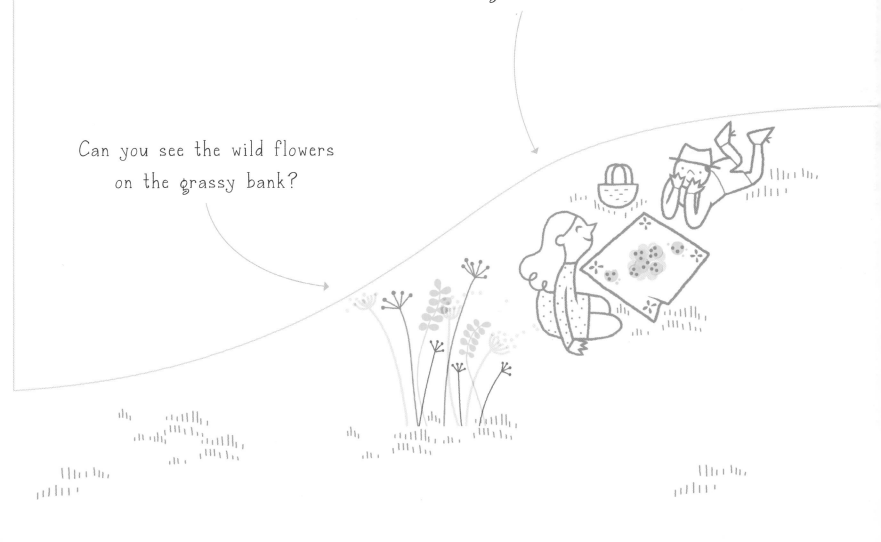

Meow!
Are these two
kittens friends?

Look at the pretty
daisies growing
in the meadow.

What color are
these flowers?

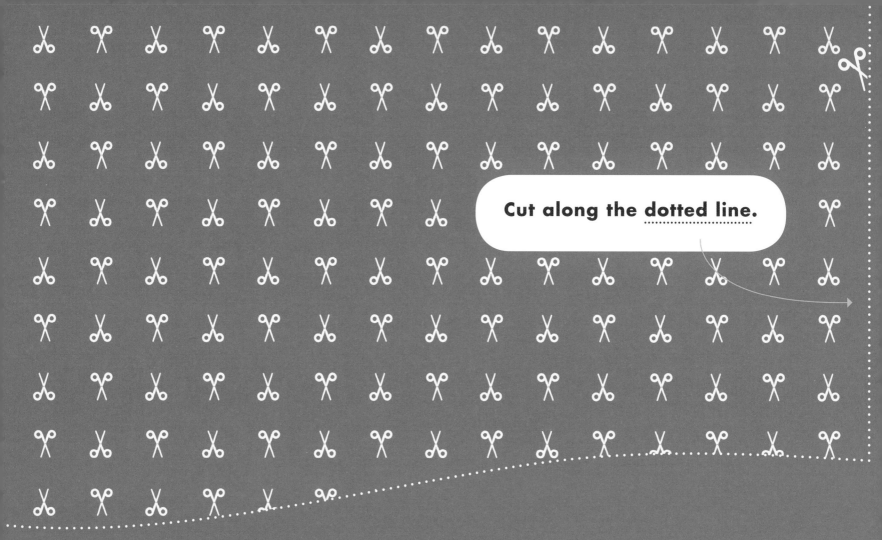

Cut along the dotted line.

How many shades of green can you use to color in these trees?

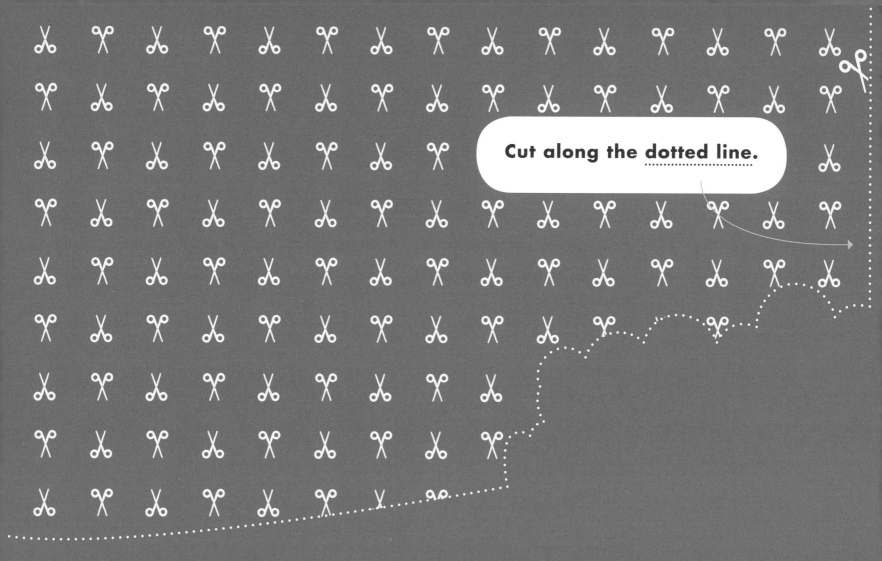

Cut along the dotted line.

Color the path a
dark brown.

Make the grass
bright green.

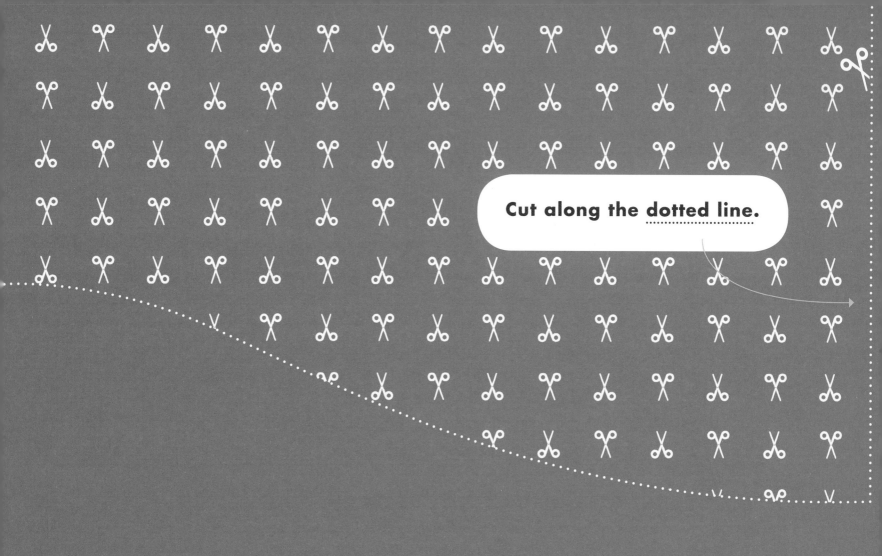

Cut along the dotted line.

SUMMER

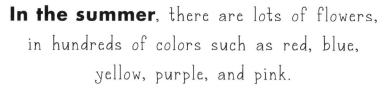

In the summer, there are lots of flowers, in hundreds of colors such as red, blue, yellow, purple, and pink.

People love to cool off in water when it gets hot, so make sure you have lots of different blue crayons ready.

Look out for brightly colored summer insects such as butterflies and dragonflies.

t is hot!

flowers, butterflies,

 make this border look

ly summery.

cutting here.

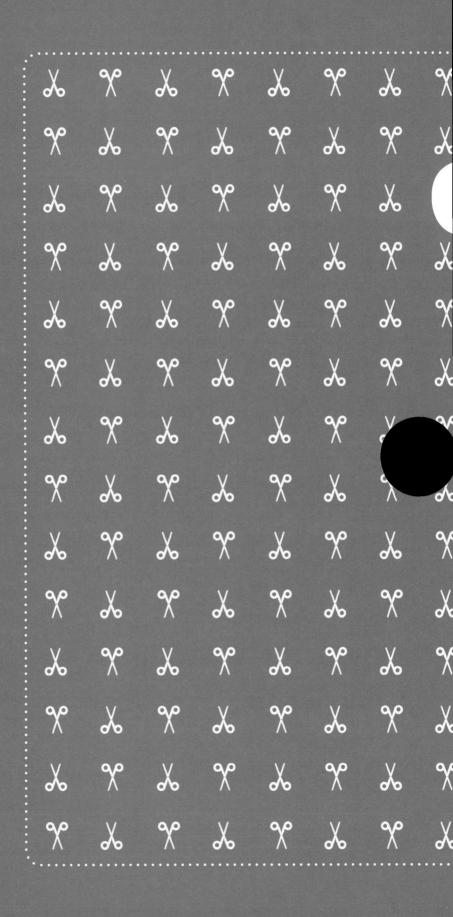

Croak croak!
A frog is hiding
in the plants.

A dragonfly is hovering by the flowers.
Its wings are a beautiful shiny blue.

Cut along the dotted line.

Shhh...
Hiding in the tall
reeds is a heron. Color it
gray and blue.

What color are
the reeds?

Cut along the dotted line, and snip
away the triangles in the bushes.

Splish splash!
The children cool off
in the water.

What color do you think
the boat should be?

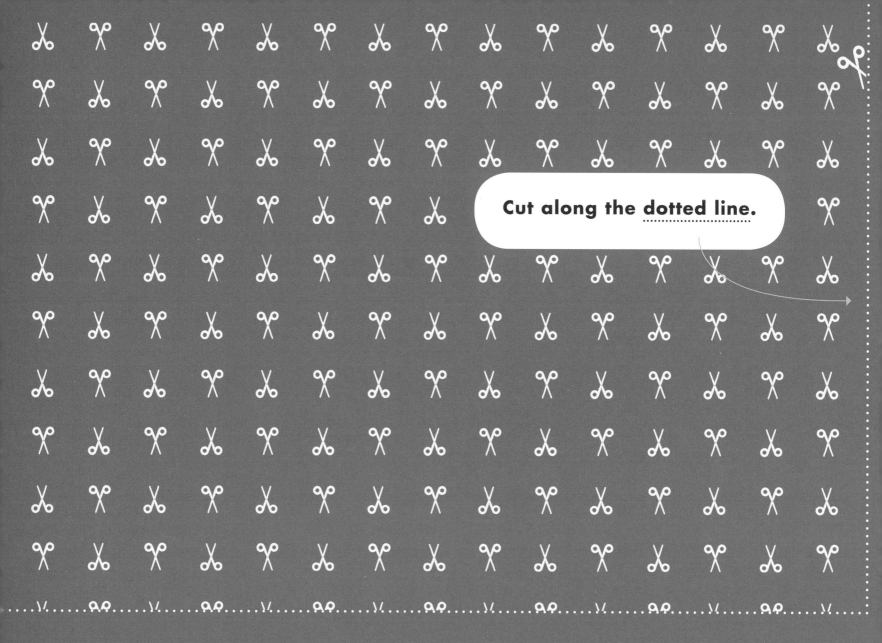

Cut along the dotted line.

Use different shades of green for these leaves.

The water is blue and calm today.

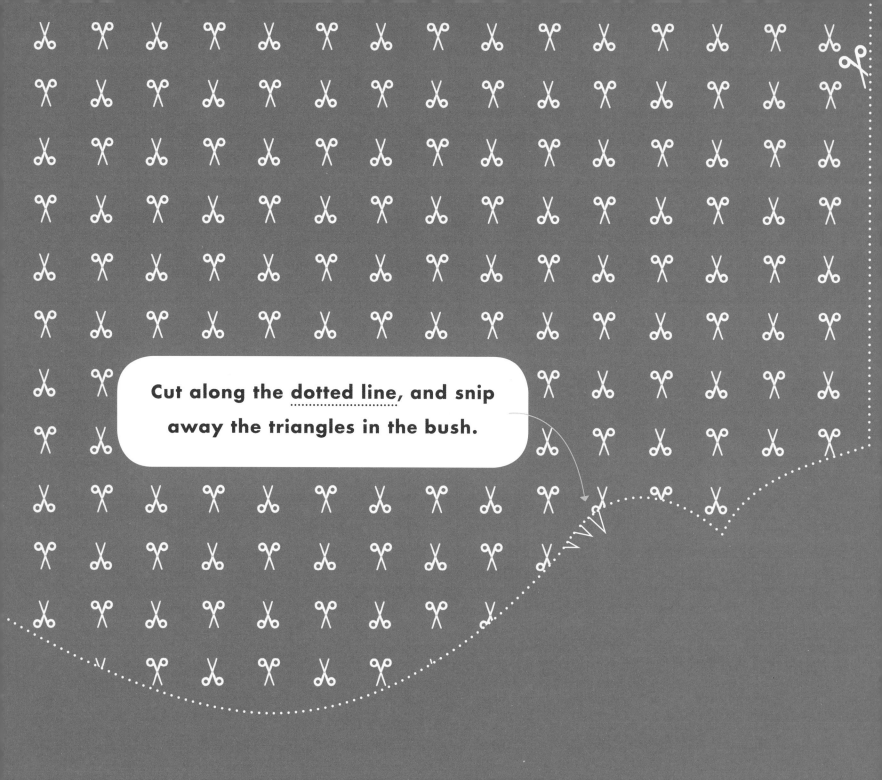

Cut along the <u>dotted line</u>, and snip away the triangles in the bush.

Phew—it's hot!
The sand is a pretty
bright yellow.

Don't forget the
pail and shovel.

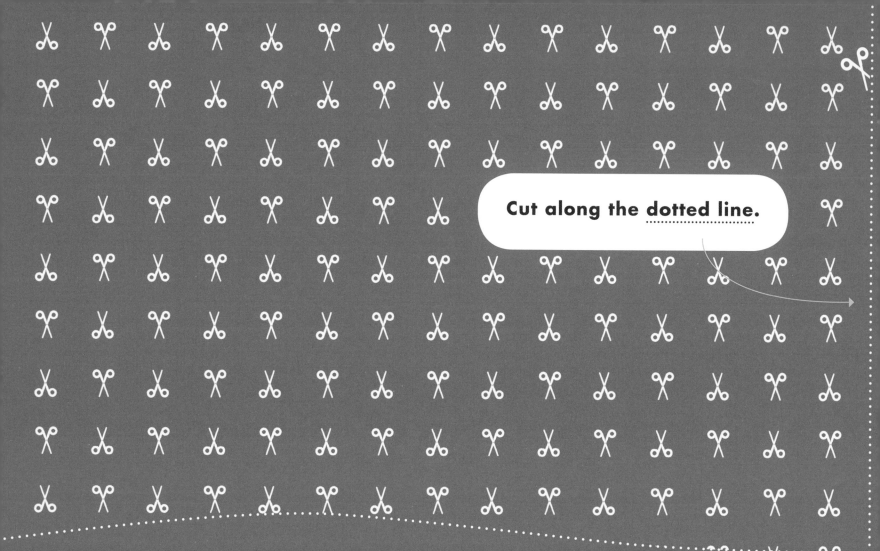

Cut along the dotted line.

What colors are
the umbrellas?

These bushes are green
and the flowers sparkle
in the sunlight.

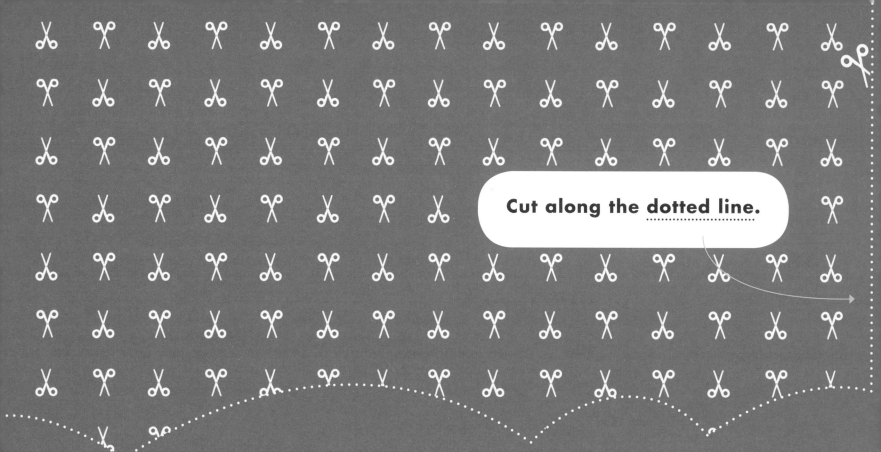

Cut along the dotted line.

Rustle rustle!

Can you see the tiny birds sheltering in the shady bush?

Cut along the **dotted line**, and snip away the triangles in the bushes.

Color the rest of
these flowers light
blue and red, too.

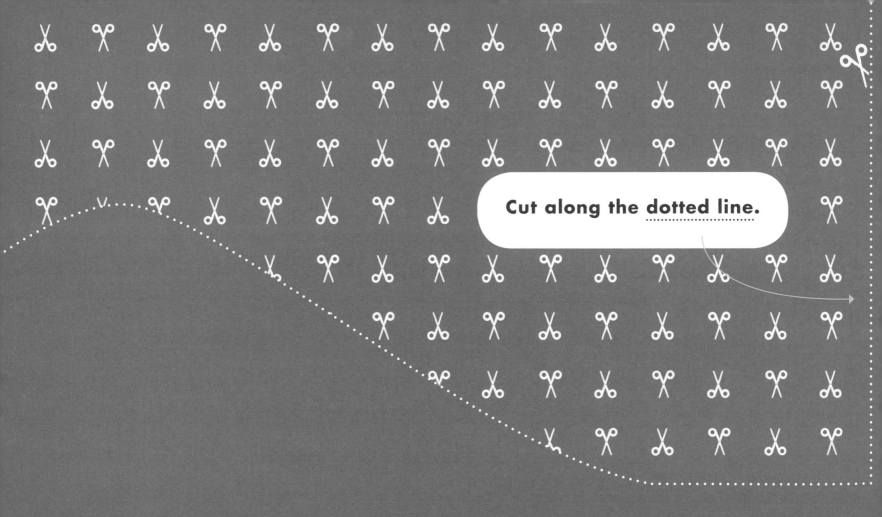

Cut along the dotted line.

FALL

In the fall, leaves on the trees turn beautiful shades of orange, red, yellow, gold, and brown.

Animals are busy finding food before the winter. See if you can find foxes, squirrels, and mice.

Look out for brightly colored mushrooms, shiny brown acorns, and blackberries.

e last season!

mushrooms, snails,

leaves to make a

per frame.

cutting here.

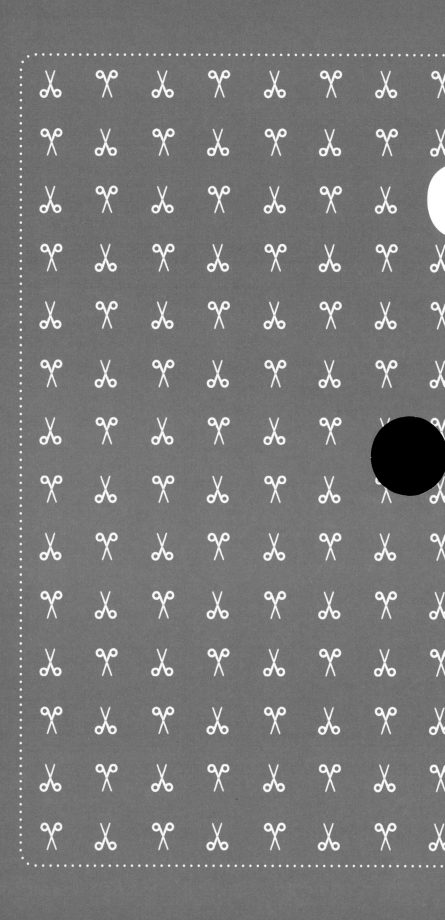

The leaves are changing color.
They are turning orange, brown,
red, yellow, and gold.

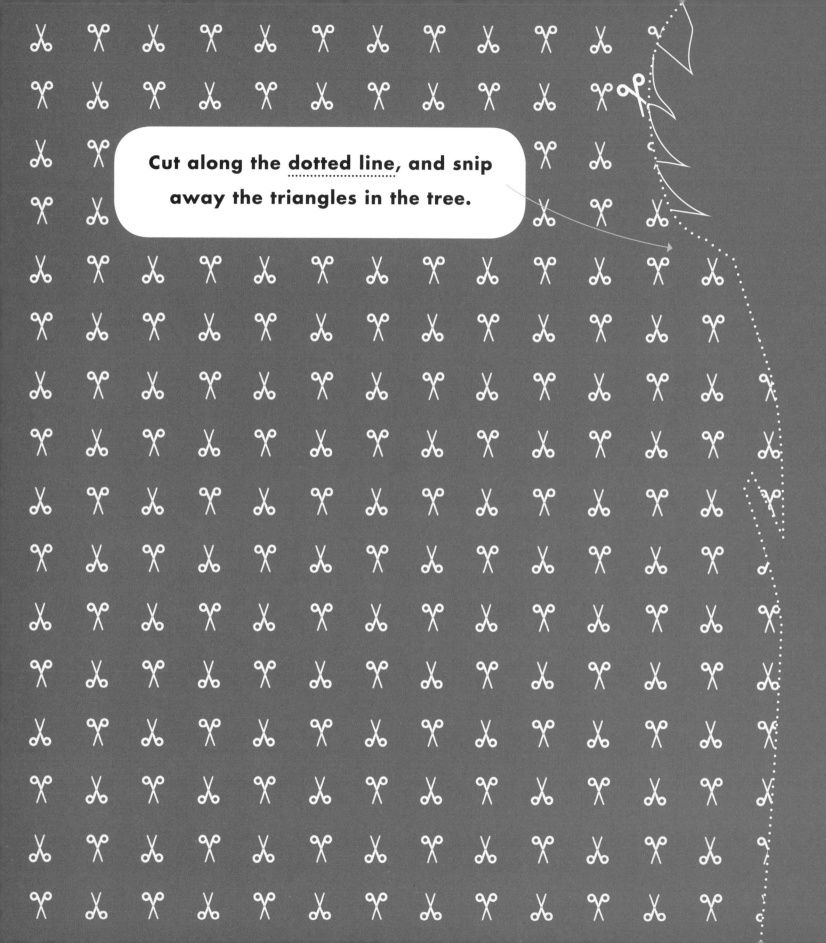

Cut along the <u>dotted line</u>, and snip away the triangles in the tree.

Slippery slowpoke!
Color the snail shells
a different color from their bodies.

Red-and-white spotted
toadstools spring up among
the fallen leaves.

Cut along the dotted line.

Quiet!

There is a fox hiding in the bushes.
Make it a reddish-brown color, but
leave its neck and tail tip white.

What colors are
the bushes?

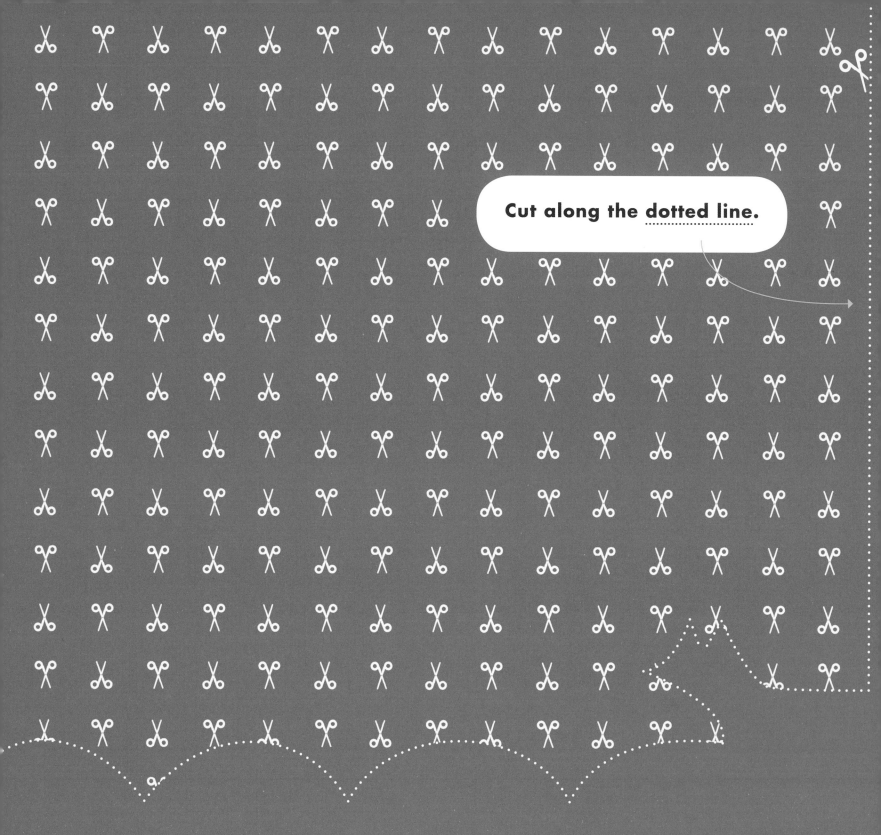

Cut along the **dotted line.**

This girl is looking for blackberries. Color her clothes using bright colors.

What color do you think her boots should be?

Cut along the dotted line, and snip away the triangles in the bush.

Color in the tree and
the leaves in browns
and oranges.

Can you see the mushrooms?
Color them red with white spots.

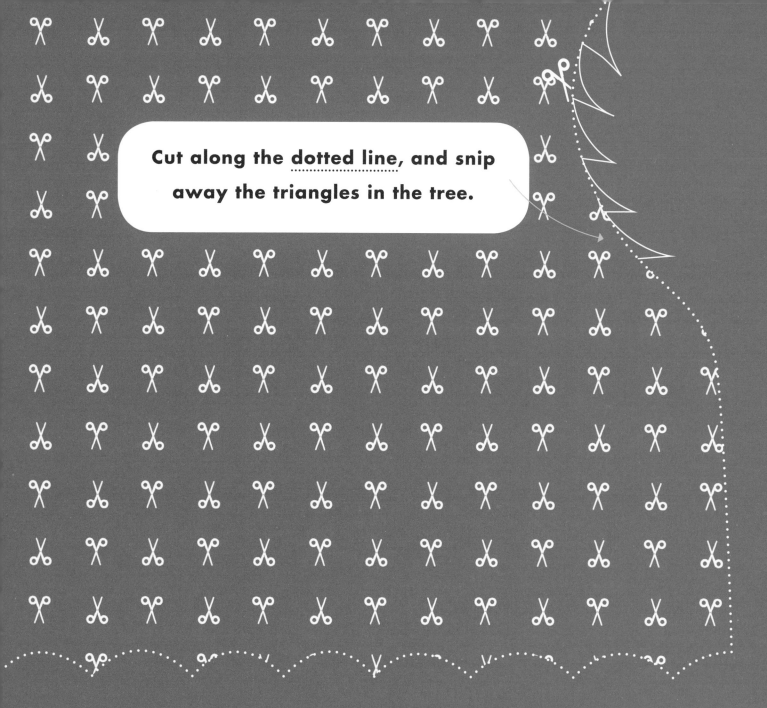

Cut along the <u>dotted line</u>, and snip away the triangles in the tree.

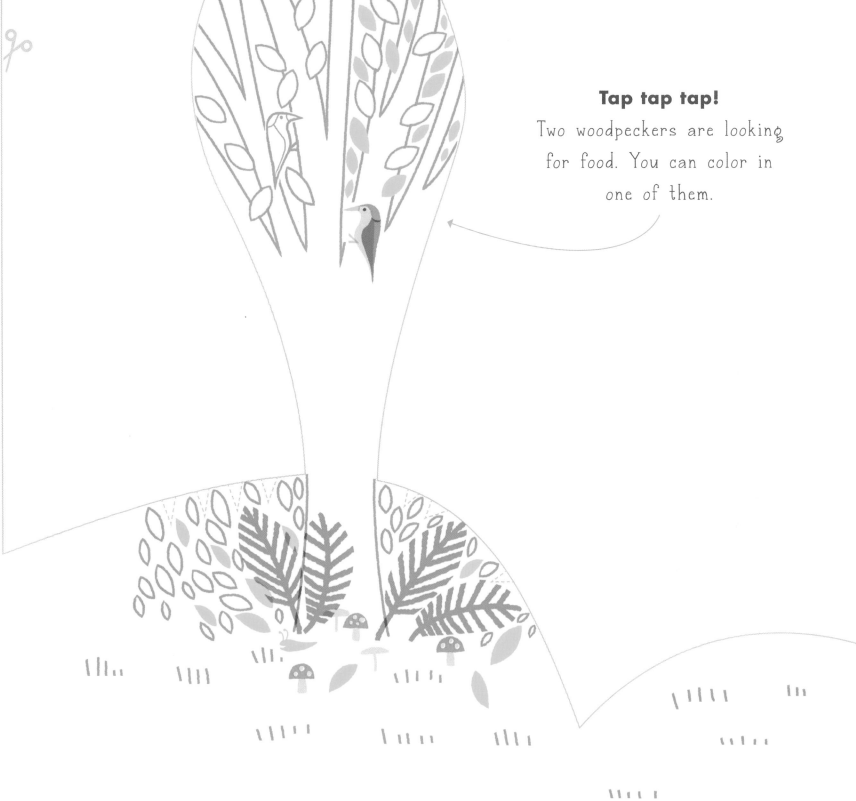

Tap tap tap!
Two woodpeckers are looking
for food. You can color in
one of them.

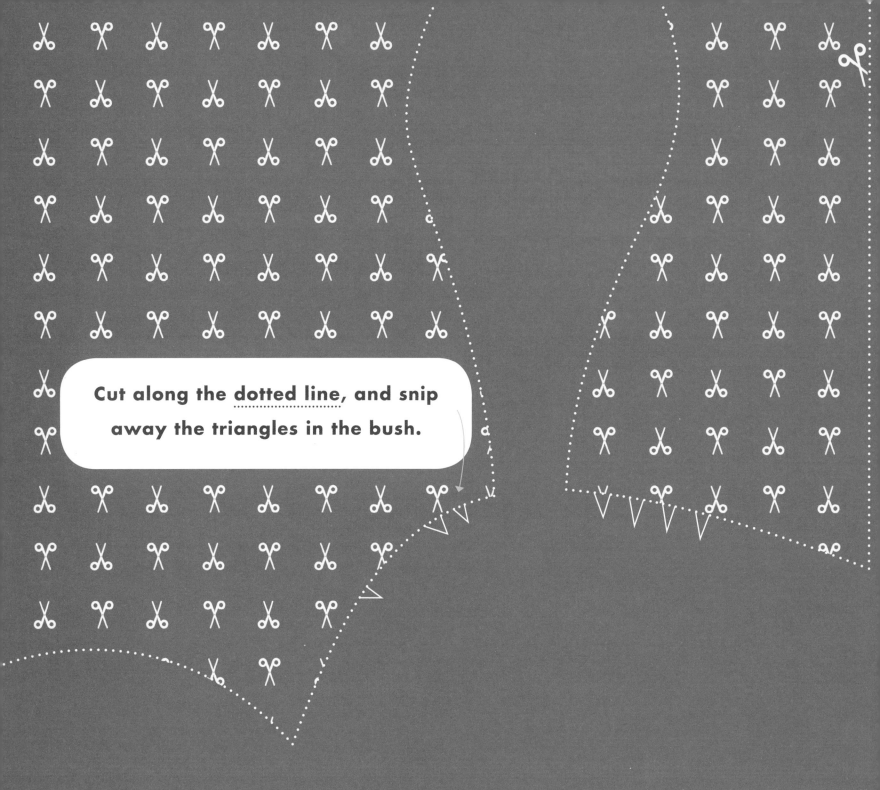

Cut along the <u>dotted line</u>, and snip away the triangles in the bush.

Can you see the mice?
Give them brown
or gray fur.

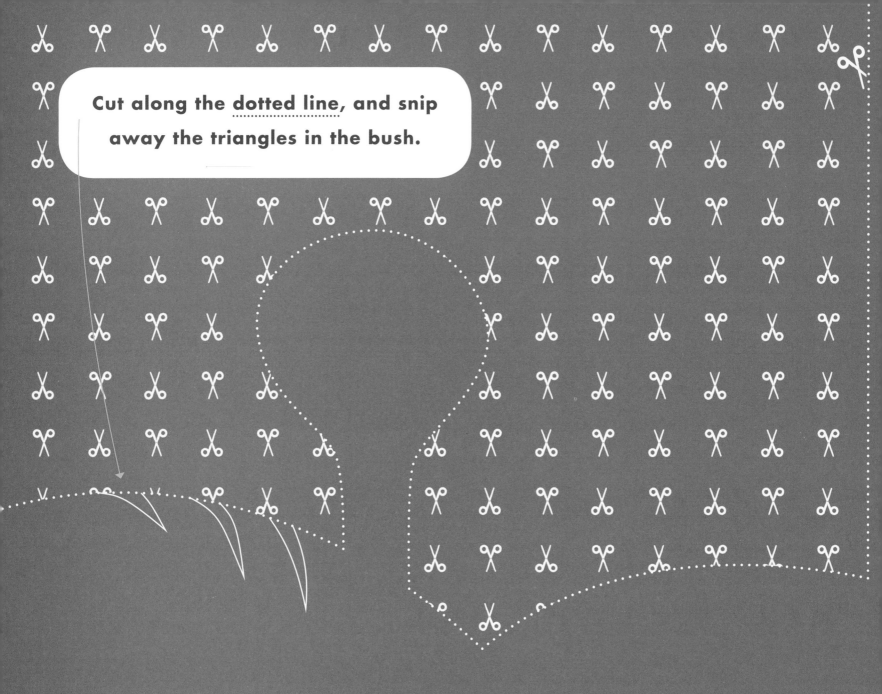

It's cloudy today.

What color are the clouds?
Is it going to rain?

Cut along the <u>dotted line</u>.

MAKE YOUR OWN THREE-LAYERED SCENE

Color, cut, and create your own mini scene

1 Decide what you would like your scene to show. It can be anything you like!

2 Draw pictures of your favorite things in the spaces shown and then color them in.

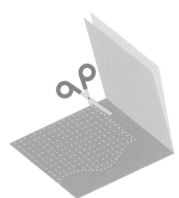

3 Turn the pages over to see what parts to cut away. Any part of the paper with the scissor pattern on it must be cut away.

4 Flip back to the frame at the front to see your very own layered picture!

Tip: Try and draw bigger things at the front and smaller things at the back.

s your frame.

der around the edge

your favorite things.

cutting here.

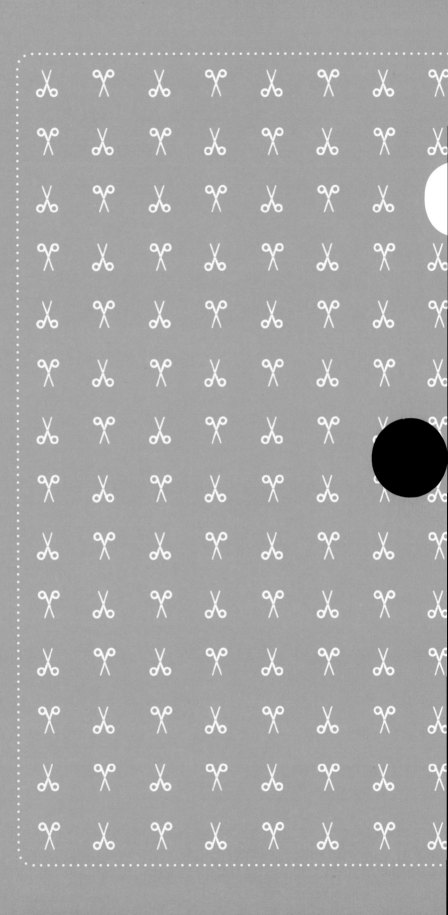

This is your first layer.

Draw something at the
bottom of the page.
This will be at the
front of your scene.

You can draw trees or bushes
on top of this line at the
edges of the scene, if you
like, but ask an adult to help
you cut them out.

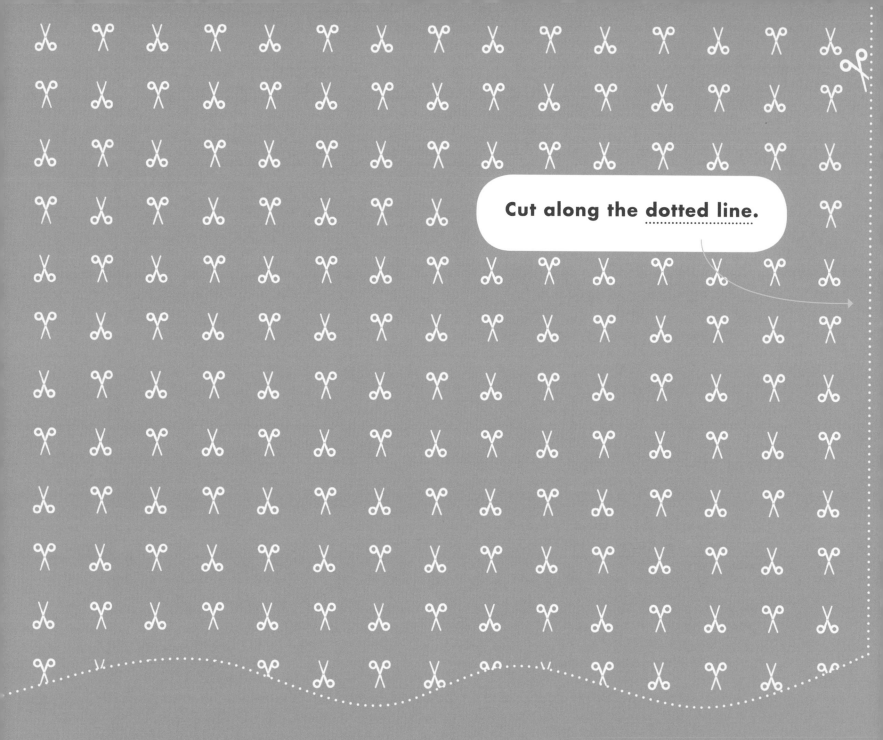

Cut along the dotted line.

This is your second layer.

Draw something in the middle of this page so you can see it above your first layer.

You can draw trees or bushes on top of this line, if you like, but ask an adult to help you cut them out.

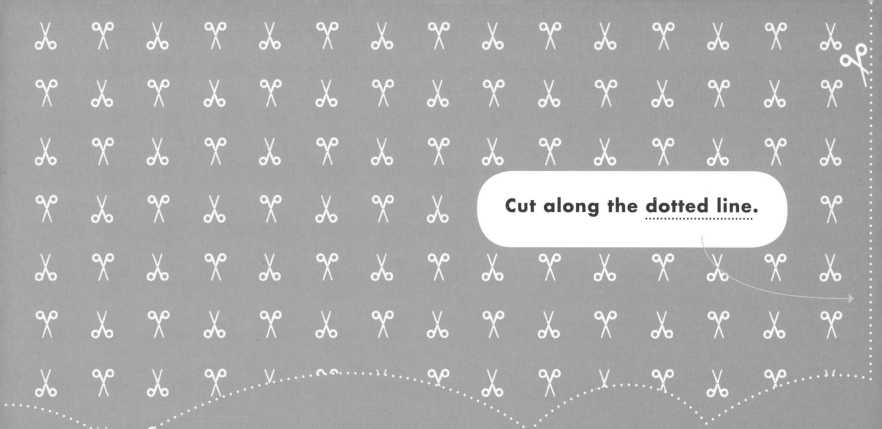

Cut along the dotted line.

**This is the back
of your scene.**
Draw something in the
top part of this page so
you can see it above
the other layers.

YOUR DESIGNS